Let's slide
into this
book ...

First Published 2025 by Jenny Dyer
For further information
Contact her through the Facebook page

Walking with Wildlife

Or on www.walkingwithwildlife.com.au

Text: © Jennifer Dyer 2025
Photography: © Jennifer Dyer 2024

ISBN 978-1-7637939-8-9

Cover and Artwork: Jenny Dyer

Walking
with Wildlife ™

BOOK 6 - A B C

Written by Jenny Dyer

Photography and Design by Jenny Dyer

A is for Ants

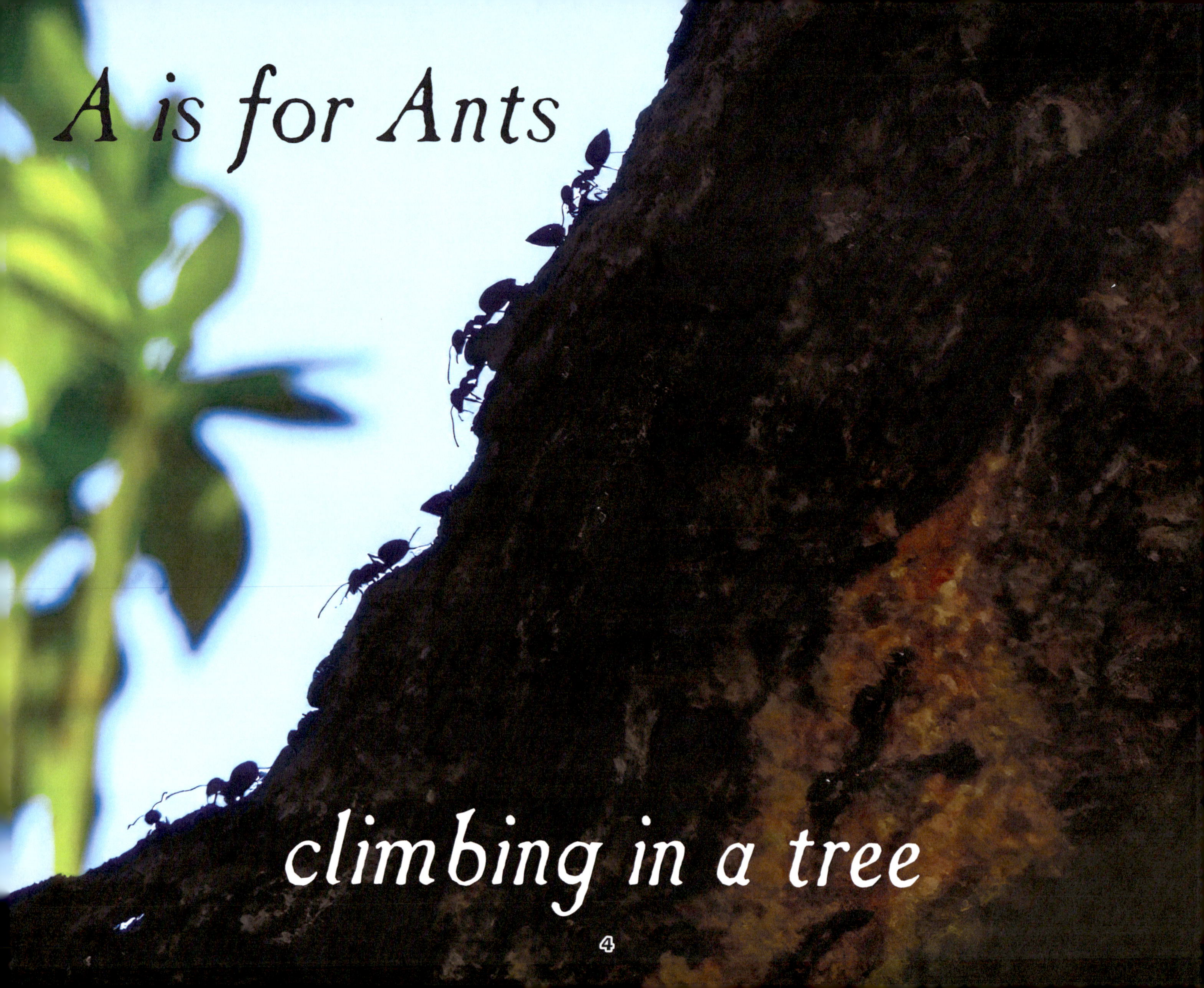

climbing in a tree

B is for bee

as busy as can be

C is for Crow

trying to catch bugs

D is for Drongo

one of nature's thugs

E is for Egret

whose neck looks hairy

_F_ is for figbird

eating a berry

G is for Grassbird

swaying on a twig

10

H is for Hare

with eyes so big

I is for Ibis

fishing at daybreak

J is for Jabiru

flying near the lake

K is for kangaroos

who fight for fun

L is for lizard

lying in the sun

M is for Magpie

singing a song

N is for nest

built so strong

O is for orb weaver

with a web to make

P is for Pelicans

swimming on the lake

Q is for Quail

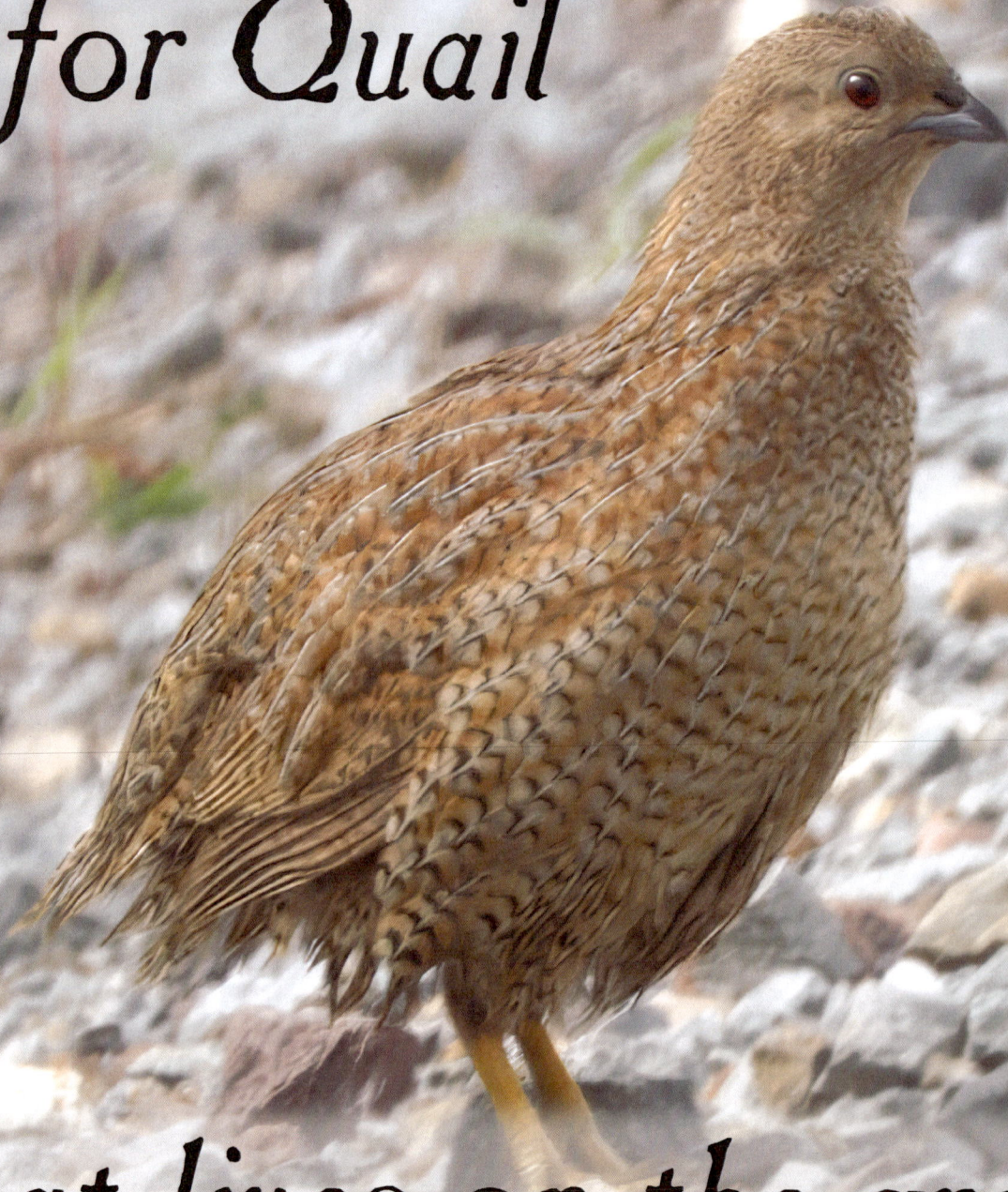

that lives on the ground

R is for Rainbow Lorikeet

that makes a loud sound

S is for snake

who's up near the eaves

T is for turkey

scratching the leaves

U is for umbrella tree

which birds love to eat

V is for variegated fairywren

with tiny little feet

W is for wasp

that stings like a bee

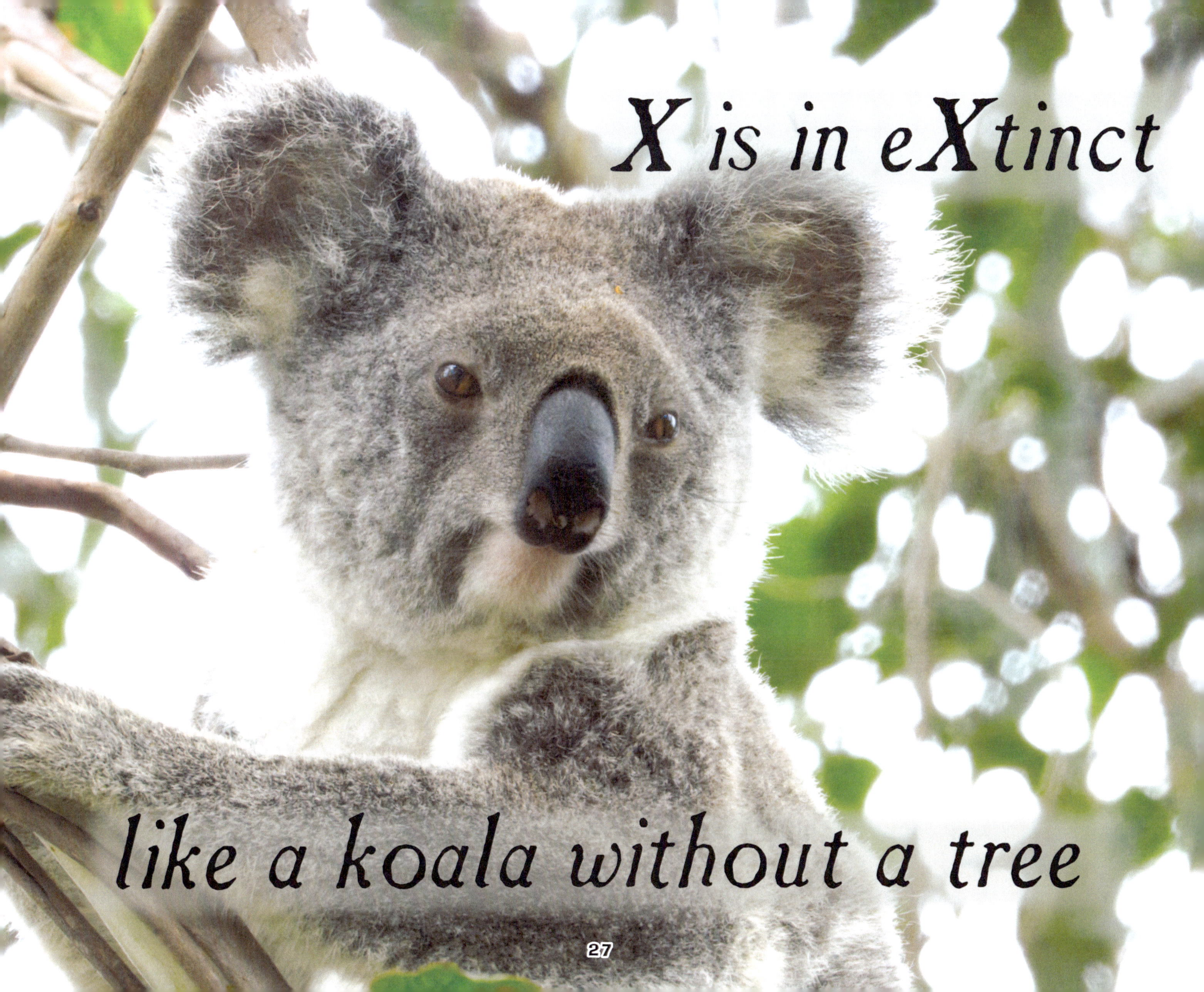

***X** is in e**X**tinct*

like a koala without a tree

Y is for Yellow Robin

hiding in a tree

Z is for Zebra Finch

singing for me

Can you name these animals or plants?

Ant

Bee

Crow

Drongo

Egret

Figbird

Grassbird

Hare

Ibis

Jabiru (Black-necked stork)

Kangaroo

Lizard (Skink)

Magpie

Can you name these animals or plants?

Nest

Orb-weaver Spider

Pelican

Quail

Rainbow Lorikeet

Snake

Turkey

Umbrella Tree

Variegated Fairywren

Wasp

Yellow Robin

Koala (nearly eXtinct)

Yellow Robin

Zebra Finch

www.ingramcontent.com/pod-product-compliance
Lightning Source LLC
Chambersburg PA
CBRC091226020426
42333CB00010B/83